Narcissism

Identifying The Patterns Of Emotional And Narcissistic Abuse And Implementing Strategies To Manage It Within Your Relationship

(Recovering From Narcissistic Abuse And Rediscovering The Self)

Randall Charest

TABLE OF CONTENT

Saving Face 1

Do You Allow The Narcissist To Exist? 10

Suggestions For Handling A Narcissist And The Effects Of Abuse 23

Recognizing The Selfish One 43

Make Use Of Externalization's Power 76

Relationship Dynamics 108

Saving Face

The concept of upholding one's social reputation, or "face," is engrained in the social structure of many Asian societies. It's not just a personal issue; it also affects family honor and social harmony and is frequently very serious. Understanding how people with narcissistic tendencies could approach this difficult topic is important when discussing narcissistic features in the context of various societies.

Certain cultures define "face" as including an individual's reputation and the reputation of their family and community. It's about maintaining social standing, harmony, and respect. Therefore, it can be seen very adversely when someone with narcissistic qualities threatens the face of himself or others.

People with narcissistic tendencies in these societies may display their traits more softly than in countries where individualism is more prominent because of the strong emphasis on face-saving. Because narcissistic conduct frequently presents as an exaggerated display of confidence or even selflessness, its subtlety can make it difficult to identify.

In these cultures, narcissistic people may go to considerable measures to hide their genuine selves to keep their faces intact. In private, they might continue to believe in their lofty self-image, but in public, they might put up a front of humility and altruism. Due to this dualism, their intimate relationships may find it extremely difficult to see through the deception and poison that lies beneath the surface.

Untangling the web of dishonesty and manipulation can be particularly difficult for people who have been in relationships with narcissists in such environments. One may ask, "Was it all just for face-saving purposes?" This uncertainty may result in perplexity and self-blame.

Now is the moment to concentrate on your journey of self-awareness. Recognizing that no one deserves to be in a toxic relationship, regardless of cultural conventions, is just as important as understanding the cultural context. You possess the ability to escape the manipulative cycle and take back control of your life.

Tough questions to pose to yourself: Do I currently belong in a poisonous relationship? Examine your relationship honestly and how it affects your mental and emotional health.

Do societal norms contribute to the concealment of narcissistic behavior? You can simplify the complexity of your experiences by realizing this.

What limits do I have? Regardless of societal norms, establish boundaries about what you will and won't accept in a relationship.

Do I need assistance and backing?

Even though the mountain can feel too big to climb, remember how satisfying healing and self-improvement are. You're moving in the right direction toward a life full of sincerity, love, and real connections by realizing the causes of narcissism and ending toxic relationships.

Face-saving does play a big role in many Asian cultures, and it can make it harder to identify narcissistic behavior. Still, everyone can find their way to self-awareness and recovery. You can empower yourself to leave toxic relationships and build a better future full of sincere connections and personal development by posing tough questions, looking for help, and comprehending the complexities of narcissism within your cultural context. Never forget that you are worthy of living a life that is real and true to who you are.

Power Dynamics and Hierarchy

Imagine this: As you move through life, you frequently get the impression that there is a power dynamic at work in your family, community, or place of employment. The perception and manifestation of narcissistic tendencies in persons operating within these hierarchies and power structures can be greatly influenced.

Power structures and cultural hierarchies resemble the unseen framework that molds our relationships and expectations. Let's dissect this even more:

People in positions of authority may be more likely to engage in selfish behavior in societies with rigid hierarchies, such as some traditional cultures or authoritarian regimes. Why? Because their sense of entitlement and superiority can be nourished by the authority heaped upon them. Consider this: It's simple to begin believing you are superior to others when you are constantly told this.

However, narcissistic qualities might not be as widely accepted or tolerated in communities with flatter power structures, where the focus is on equality and collaboration. These cultures may promote a more humble and community-focused way of living, which inhibits the growth of narcissistic tendencies.

This is where things become intriguing: Our cultural background frequently influences our perception of narcissistic conduct. These actions could be viewed as ambitious or self-assured in cultures that uphold hierarchical power structures and occasionally even as admirable. In these settings, it's not unusual for people to confuse arrogance with confidence.

However, narcissistic tendencies are more likely to be seen negatively in societies where power relationships are flatter. Here, cooperation and humility are valued, and people who exhibit extreme conceit or a lack of empathy are frequently shunned or condemned.

Do You Allow The Narcissist To Exist?

Have you ever found yourself in a position where you can see that a relationship is toxic, but nobody else can? When someone exhibits poisonous behaviors, do those around you also fail to see them? And others who fail to recognize the poisoning say, "Just let it go." Families apologize. Keep it out of your mind. She doesn't mean it at all.

You give opportunities as a result of listening to what people around you are saying. You also extend a free pass. Unfortunately, poisonous people's actions go unpunished. Everyone in your immediate vicinity keeps defending the individual. While you sit there in total stillness, perplexed by what you see.

Everyone else carries on with their lives in the interim. People ignore it. They excuse these kinds of actions. Furthermore, the poisonous individual, the narcissist, will not alter since they cannot recognize how their actions are harming other people.

Narcissists see silence as permission to continue their poisonous behavior since they are not confronted for it. This is regarded as giving the narcissist permission to carry on acting in this manner toward other people. We live in a world of second chances, let's face it. We like to think that individuals can change things and make a difference.

Too often, we give them the benefit of the doubt.

Giving decent people a second opportunity is perfectly acceptable because they can change their behavior and character. Giving the narcissists another chance, meanwhile, is akin to permitting them to carry on with their behaviors. The field of addictions is where the term "enabling" is most frequently employed. When someone brings booze or drugs to an addict, they are essentially giving them unspoken permission to continue consuming.

How does this apply to the field of narcissism? We do, inadvertently, carry on providing the narcissist with a narcissistic supply in silence. When we allow someone to carry on with their bad routines and behaviors, we give them more power. By not enforcing consequences for inappropriate behavior, we can facilitate the behavior alternatively when we do nothing but watch helplessly while these narcissists harm others.

If you don't believe someone who is a narcissist victim, you are also viewed as supporting the narcissist. Giving opportunities and forgiving others are narcissistic tools for narcissists. The more you offer the narcissist forgiveness and chances, the more you enable the destructive behavior to persist.

Attempting to please and appease a narcissist out of fear of confronting them is another approach to enable a narcissist. We let them do everything they want, for example, and we let them always decide where to eat. Recall that giving in to pressure is giving in. In any type of narcissistic relationship, we are enabled when we put up with someone. If you don't want to disturb a narcissist in an intimate relationship, you may enable them by letting go of issues or by keeping your sentiments to yourself.

It occurs when you keep approving of their actions and their unfavorablereactions. When a narcissist advances in the corporate world, this occurs because no one wants to kill the golden goose. The harsh actions of a narcissist are interpreted as forceful, and their sense of entitlement is seen as confident. Numerous mechanisms encourage and reward these tendencies as toxic leaders increase.

Regretfully, you will be the one used as a scapegoat and gaslighted if you expose the narcissist in public. Now, the situation is: observe something, say nothing. Because our culture tolerates and even celebrates narcissistic behavior, narcissism is on the rise. We allow leaders of many organizations and establishments to get away with it. Additionally, we permit inconsiderate influencers and celebrities to get away with it.

Giving the narcissist genuine consequences is the only way to end their enabling behavior, but this is difficult to accomplish. Because that is precisely what the narcissist wants:

Stop complimenting them and stop showing up where they are.

Give them no more audience support or applause for their accomplishments when they feel validated.

Shut off the air source!

It is that easy, but it's really difficult to do.

The Effects of Narcissism on Oneself and Relationships

With all of its many effects, narcissism has a significant impact on relationships as well as an individual's sense of self. Managing connections with a narcissistic person has an impact on people's identity and emotional health in addition to the immediate interpersonal dynamics.

A pervasive feeling of unbalance frequently typifies narcissism's effects on relationships. Because of their constant need for approval and self-validation, narcissists may put their own goals and ambitions ahead of their partners'. A relationship that lacks empathy and reciprocity may result from this self-centeredmindset. Because of this, the non-narcissistic spouse could experience feelings of being ignored, undervalued, or pressured to live up to the narcissist's continually shifting demands.

Moreover, a poisonous dynamic is exacerbated by the manipulative characteristics that are intrinsic to narcissistic conduct. There are many different ways that manipulation can occur, from covert emotional blackmail to overt gaslighting. While the narcissist belittles their confidence and tries to dictate the course of the relationship, the non-narcissistic partner may go through perplexity, self-doubt, and a warped perception of reality. This gradually undermines trust and fosters an unstable emotional atmosphere.

One of the most important aspects of managing narcissism in relationships is the effect on self-esteem. The narcissistic partner's continued demand for outside approval can cause the other person to feel less valuable. Recurring feelings of being undervalued or underappreciated can reduce self-assurance and an increased susceptibility to emotional manipulation. The spouse who is not narcissistic could doubt their judgment and value, creating an internal conflict that might last long after the relationship ends.

Under severe circumstances, a narcissistic partner's emotional abuse might result in "narcissistic abuse syndrome." Post-traumatic stress disorder, depression, anxiety, and other psychological and emotional effects are all included in this condition. The person could struggle to set limits, have trouble trusting people, and battle feelings of guilt and shame.

Narcissism affects a person's sense of self in ways that go beyond relationships. Keeping up a grandiose façade becomes a coping strategy for those with narcissistic features to protect their fragile self-esteem. A shallow and erratic sense of self-identity might arise from an ongoing need for approval and achievement from others. Underneath the outward confidence, inadequacies and a dread of being discovered frequently lurk beneath the surface.

Furthermore, chasing idealistic ideals of power, beauty, or success might leave one dissatisfied with reality. People with narcissistic qualities may be motivated by this discontent to take risks or make flimsy connections toto prove their value. Their unrealistic expectations of themselves and their real accomplishments or relationships don't match, which can lead to a never-ending cycle of dissatisfaction and disappointment.

In summary, narcissism has a wide-ranging and complex effect on relationships and the self. Relationship imbalance, manipulation, and emotional abuse from narcissists can have long-lasting psychological effects and lower one's sense of self-worth. Understanding these dynamics is essential for people managing these relationships and reconstructing their identities after that. Moreover, educating people on the complexity of narcissism is crucial to developing empathy and offering assistance to people impacted by these difficult dynamics.

Suggestions For Handling A Narcissist And The Effects Of Abuse

It's crucial to go over some of the main signs that you are experiencing narcissistic abuse syndrome before discussing tips for coping with narcissists and the fallout from abuse.

The overwhelming sense that you are alone is the first and most important clue that you are in a toxic relationship with a narcissist. You may be dealing with a narcissist who is merely giving you a false impression of the relationship you thought you were in if you see your boyfriend every day when you get home, eat meals with him or her, watch TV with him or her, and go to bed next to him or her, but you still feel like you've spent the entire day alone. Beneath the behaviors that leave you feeling disoriented, bewildered, and incredibly alone, there is an absence of feeling. Narcissistic abuse syndrome may be present if you experience this regularly and you don't know why.

You might have narcissistic abuse syndrome if you are always troubled by the notion that you are just not good enough for anyone, particularly your boyfriend or spouse. Narcissists are skilled in undermining their victims' sense of self-worth and persuading them—through deceptive and overt means—that they are incompetent, prone to errors, etc. They could laugh at you, tease you, or make you feel insignificant. You get the impression from this abuse that you are unworthy and that you will never be able to achieve anything in life.

As your narcissistic partner tries to take control of your personal life and all that was there before they joined your life, you could feel as though the relationship is suffocating you. Isolating the victim from those they formerly trusted and loved is a standard tactic used by those in control to maintain control over them. A narcissist aims to become the sole person you can depend on for any form of assistance.

A further indicator of narcissistic abuse syndrome is realizing that your essential beliefs, values, ideals, or other qualities have changed, making you a different person. Suppose your partner has altered these fundamental aspects of who you are, and it doesn't seem right. In that case, there may be toxic forces at play in your relationship that are working hard to transform you into someone who solely benefits the narcissist.

Outright name-calling is a common tactic used by narcissists to undermine their victim's sense of self-worth. The narcissist may initially present this behavior as a joke or jest rather than as an overt behavior. "You're just overreacting because you're too sensitive," he would chuckle. These remarks could initially appear benign, but if said repeatedly, the victim may eventually internalize them to the point where the allegations become true. They might begin to believe these beliefs, even though initially, they didn't think they were negatively impacting them.

Ultimately, the "hurt and rescue" cycle can cause a victim to suffer from emotional anxiety and problems for the rest of their life. Using this tactic, the narcissist puts the victim under stress by bringing up an incident, a disagreement, or an accusation, after which they give them silent treatment for a predetermined period. The goal is to reduce that stress or silence it for a while. Therefore, they might employ a different strategy than the silent treatment. When applied in this manner, the silent treatment awakens an underlying fear of abandonment in almost everyone. Thus, as long as the victim experiences attachment and emotion towards the offender, it becomes an unavoidable tactic to cause suffering.

The victim has learned to be scared anytime the cycle recurs, anticipating that moment of staged abandonment or stillness. The rescue stage involves the perpetrator returning and decreasing the victim's fear of abandonment.

Because the emotions connected to desertion may be so intense and painful, this tactic eventually becomes a potent behavior manipulation and control method. We are all hardwired to need attention, love, and affection, so when someone gives it to us and then abruptly withdraws it, we learn to do whatever it takes to keep that attachment from vanishing—even if it means apologizing, much to the narcissist's delight, for something we didn't even do.

If you suspect that someone in your intimate connection is a narcissist, you should receive help leaving as soon as you can. Learn the strategies employed by narcissists to maintain the attachment-based feeling within you and make every effort to refuse and escape. Tell yourself that nothing you felt linked to was true and that this was all an act.

Your best line of defense when dealing with a narcissist who is not your love partner but is nevertheless an inevitable presence in your life is going to be your ongoing knowledge of any tricks and manipulation the narcissist may try to pull on you. Since the narcissist's entire existence is focused on harming other people, it would be foolish to launch an all-out attack on him. He will undoubtedly be able to devote more time and emotional energy to hurting you than you will to injuring him. You're not that kind of person, anyway!

Even though you might be angry, the narcissist wants you to let your guard down and lose control, so resist the urge to give in to his demands.

Strength in numbers is a nice general rule, as always. Get assistance from others and create a barrier if you feel exposed or susceptible to a narcissist in your vicinity. Tell the narcissist that you won't give an inch and that you are too intelligent to fall for his tricks. Put on a thick skin and get ready for hurtful remarks that make you angry. You are not required to succumb to this. Create a support network and carry on with your life. The narcissist will look elsewhere and leave you alone once he realizes you've pretty much become resistant to his charms. Keep an eye out for anyone else you believe he could be targeting, and alert them to the situation if you believe they are also at risk. This will likely set off a defensive reaction, but it's important to keep cool and remember who you are and your situation. Refuse to believe the narcissist when he presents himself as someone he is not. He is just a shy little child trying to find validation in the admiration of others. You and the people you care about are not under his control. You are stronger than this individual since you know the strength and power of true love and affection.

We'll talk about some suggestions and guidance for people who have experienced narcissistic abuse and are working toward recovery in our last chapter. We will also explore how you might arm yourself against future narcissist abuse. As always, I urge you to learn everything you can about the narcissist and his many scams. After all, power comes from knowledge.

Manipulation and Additional Narcissistic Patterns and Attributes

The need for affirmation from others drives a narcissist. When they don't obtain this, they turn to manipulation as coercion to get approval or adoration from others.

Trickery

A person can manipulate another person unfairly, cunningly, or dishonestly by using a manipulative deed or instrument. One of a narcissist's most frequently utilized tools is this one. They get the sensation of power they want by manipulating other people. Various manipulation strategies are employed by narcissists based on their objectives:

Gaslighting: When you question their acts or conduct, they will say things like "You imagined it" or "It did not happen."

Generalizations: They won't genuinely examine or consider your point of view. They take one component and apply it to your entire mental process.

Projection: They never accept responsibility for anything and always blame you.

Changing the topic: They will do this repeatedly until they are seen in a favorable light if you are discussing something they see as bad or threatening to their warped reality.

Shifting the goalposts: This tactic ensures that others never meet or refute the narcissist's expectations.

Smear campaigns: This phrase is commonly used in the media to describe political campaigns in which two candidates attempt to discredit the other by spreading untrue or inflated claims. When narcissists try to dictate how you see them and yourself, they will act similarly.

Calling someone names is a typical tactic to silence any criticism they may receive.

Aggressive jokes: These are meant to make fun of and denigrate other people, but they are disguised as humor to give the impression that the narcissist is not being cruel.

Devaluation: This is done to give them a sense of increased authority. Your self-esteem may suffer as a result, which gives the narcissist more power over you.

Another tactic used to exert control and authority over an individual is triangulation. The narcissist will tell you that other people are speaking about negative things. This will take your mind off of the nasty things the narcissist is giving you.

haughtiness

This is an overblown belief in one's significance or skills. One of the most prevalent characteristics of narcissists is this. The narcissist acts in this way because they want to be regarded as the most valuable and admirable person in the world. They believe that their viewpoints and methods are the only correct ones. Here are some indicators that someone is arrogant:

The individual is constantly self-promoting, saying and doing things to enhance their appearance.

Any attempt to refute their worldview will make them defensive.

Their interactions are tumultuous. For instance, they might say they no longer like someone after being friends for a while.

They treat those different from them adversely.

They exude a fake charm and aren't afraid to reveal how vicious they can be, even to the people they say they care about the most.

They are particularly harsh and illogical in their criticism of others.

When it comes to friendships, they value quantity more than quality.

Unreal or Overstated Achievement

Never will a narcissist acknowledge defeat. They put forth effort to present themselves as more accomplished and successful than they are. They frequently fabricate this misleading impression by overlooking or lying about their achievements. For instance, they might buy a costly car they cannot afford or an apartment that is much beyond their means to appear more successful. It all comes down to projecting an image that corresponds with their feeling of grandeur and fantasy.

Failed Relationships

Relationships and narcissism don't go together. A genuine and mutually beneficial connection is impossible to maintain with a selfish person. They'll declare their affection and concern for you. They can be incredibly charming and charismatic when they think it would be advantageous to them. They can switch between seeming aloof and careless one moment and charming the next. Those they are in relationships with may become quite confused and suffer emotional injury as a result of this. Despite their charm, they might say that their partner never supports them. This may occur even after a brief interval during which they are not fully focused. Of course, part of their relationship problems also involve their apologizing and making changes and promises. They may sound extremely convincing when they say such things, but they are not being genuine.

Exaggerating

A person with narcissistic tendencies lives in fantasy. Their lifestyles are not real, grounded in reality. They imagine the life they desire, then employ exaggeration and other strategies to give the impression that their vision of the ideal life is what they are truly living. When someone challenges and uncovers their delusion, they struggle to cope.

Telling stories is one of the traits of narcissists. They consider the details, allowing them to tell an authentic story. They feel strong and in command when they narrate their stories. They are not hesitant to take advantage of or manipulate others to satisfy their fantasies or give them what they desire to keep their fantasy alive.

A narcissist's behavior tends to get more obvious and intense as they age. Their behavior usually reaches its peak when they reach their 40s or 50s. Nevertheless, their actions can make them unpredictable regardless of their age. Getting them to act badly or express strong, unfavorable feelings like abrupt, overwhelming rage doesn't take much.

Recognizing The Selfish One

Not every conceited or boastful person is a narcissist. Each of us possesses some of the features listed in the preceding chapter, but that doesn't automatically make us all narcissists. Being able to identify the narcissist in your life is crucial because they have the potential to bring emotional or even physical harm to you. The narcissist has no regrets and will take advantage of or harm other people. For him, nothing matters more than his benefit.

The narcissist will bare his teeth or reveal his wicked nature when he feels—that is, thinks—that he is not getting the respect, love, or devotion he so desperately seeks. Usually, the person who loves him the most will end up suffering. When faced with challenging circumstances, a narcissist may become erratic in their mood, engage in extramarital affairs, take drugs, turn to alcohol, become violent or verbally abusive, or engage in other harmful and improper activities.

You might be in a relationship with a narcissist if there is something about your partner that bothers, unnerves, or shames you, and you are reluctant to disclose it to even your closest friends and family. While regular boasting may irritate you to some extent, the narcissist will inflict more emotional distress or agony than usual.

Particularly the covert narcissist, narcissists are adept at concealing who they are. However, if you're alert, you may recognize him in various settings and save yourself much pain. The overt narcissist's narcissistic qualities are simple to spot; with the covert narcissist, you have to be more watchful and vigilant.

Having a relationship with a narcissist

He gives you a lot of love and attention.

The fact that he is obsessed with you may excite you. He never stops praising you and showering you with likes on Facebook, texts, calls, flowers, and gifts. It all seems too much, too soon, and maybe it is. Be cautious because scammers and narcissists frequently use this tactic to get you into their webs (see "love bombing" in Chapter 5).

He's slick and engaging.

He is an expert at seducing his prey because of his experience and predatory tendencies. He'll pretend to be your prince charming to trick you.

He makes the moon his pledge.

The narcissist enjoys making lofty claims to demonstrate what a wonderful person he is, especially when witnesses are present. He frequently forgets or doesn't intend to follow his promises, so give it time and observe whether he does.

He sets aside his former partner.

He speaks poorly of all the previous women he has dated and labels her as a cunning gold-digger. Then, to gain your love, he tells you you are unique. The narcissist usually assigns blame or responsibility to others for their errors; he seldom takes ownership of his blunders. He might also point the finger at his supervisor, father, coworkers, etc. He'll try to play the victim to gain your compassion.

He shows his mother either passionate love or severe hate.

The narcissist's primary caregiver may also be one. Typically, the child's relationship with the narcissistic parent is poisonous, marked by love and hatred.

He mentions names.

He teasingly tosses out the names of well-known people he knows to impress you without appearing arrogant. He may also talk about his accomplishments, travels, and possessions. He's putting on a show to make it easier for you to fall in love with him.

He treats the waitress badly.

Those that the narcissist doesn't feel obligated to impress may be the target of his entitlement complex and lack of empathy. He might use deception or threats to secure a seat without reservation or make fun of the waiter (or the cabbie, the front desk clerk, the valet, etc.) over a minor transgression.

He has too much power.

Men who can make wise decisions and know when to order wine or food on a date tend to impress women. However, the narcissist won't take into account your wants or even inquire as to what you desire.

He's in a hurry.

He pushes you into a relationship or into having sex too quickly; he might even propose marriage. Does he discuss plans for the future of the two of you and having kids too soon into the relationship? The narcissist is impatient because he can't maintain his pretense for very long.

Early in the relationship is the ideal time to end things. Never believe that you can influence a narcissist. He is unable to change since his problems are too entrenched. Save yourself the agony and cruelty and get out while you still can.

The conceited Companion

His initial demeanor is one of charm and friendliness.

When someone has something he wants, the narcissist will use his charm to make friends with them. He will change from his initial pleasant demeanor when he gets what he wants.

There's a posse surrounding him.

The narcissist only has friends who help him achieve his goals; he has no true pals. In his life, his supposed companions are acquaintances who come and go. When they can no longer meet his wants, he quickly departs them and finds new.

"friends."

It's difficult to confide in him about your worries or secrets.

He will make fun of you, put you down, or show you no sympathy if you try to open up to him. He can't give back when needed, even though you were there for him when he was down.

He's counting on you to share his opinion on everything.

He won't tolerate it if you disagree with him and might even shame or ignore you in return.

You'll always be the supporting cast member.

The narcissist will never let you share the spotlight. He will be the center of attention in everything. He'll control the conversation and draw all the focus to himself.

There will be an uneasy feeling regarding your friendship.

You won't always know what it is, but dealing with a narcissist will make you feel violated, used, or disturbed. That's because his manipulation of you to suit his demands is your friendship's foundation.

Indices That Point to a Narcissistic Partnership

You soon start to exhibit unmistakable symptoms of an abuse victim when you are subjected to various kinds of abuse regularly. Not everyone will display every single symptom on the list or follow this same pattern, and not having any of these symptoms does not always indicate that the victim is not being abused. Familiarize yourself with this list so you can spot abuse in either yourself or in others.

The indicators listed below will assist you in identifying the painful bond that results from being in a narcissistic relationship.

Your Speech Is Not Heard

Narcissists frequently muffle your voice since they are only interested in themselves, especially if you have empathy. It may not begin violently at first, but over time, you will notice that your words and emotions are no longer important and that this larger-than-life character suddenly occupies the centerof your universe while you are left with no voice. When you lose your voice, your once-observant friends and family will label you as acting "strange" since you aren't the same person you once were.

An Illusory Relationship Picture

It is simpler for you to fabricate a false picture of your connection and to defend the narcissist's problems when you are with them. You deceive yourself into believing you are bonded to the person, even when others can see you are having difficulties in the relationship. This will facilitate the abuse and poison to persist.

Controlling and Manipulative Actions

Because it's the only way they can maintain control over everyone else and exert dominance over others, narcissists also aim to manipulate other people's conduct in addition to their self-interest.

Unrelentingly Negative and Contained Feelings

You won't be able to express what you want to say in a relationship with a narcissist because everything about the relationship is focused on feeding this person's ego and opinions, and you will always be silenced.

A person becomes less emotionally expressive when emotions are suppressed for an extended period. This leads to doubts, concerns, phobias, and poor self-confidence, undermining the individual's belief in the connection.

You often feel down or unhappy.

Being in a happy relationship should bring you joy. Suppose you regularly experience sadness and depression in your relationship, and you are unable to link these emotions to anything outside of it. In that case, it might be time to examine the reasons behind your sentiments in-depth. Even if you are unable to identify the abusive acts, you might be able to identify how you feel, which could indicate that your unhappiness and melancholy are the result of emotional abuse.

Self-doubt and Pointing

You might even start to hold yourself responsible for the narcissist's abuse, telling yourself that you irritated them, that's why they punched you, and that if you are more cautious going forward, it won't happen. You hold the narcissist accountable for your actions, which only serves to persuade you that the abuse was OK and that you deserved it.

You're not as happy with your achievements.

The narcissist will minimize your accomplishments while highlighting theirs. Things that used to make you feel proud or joyful may no longer make you feel that way, which could be an indication that you have been the victim of narcissistic abuse. The issue with this kind of abuse is that you could unconsciously admire your partner, making it difficult for you to recognize the phrase as abuse. Just remember that you should feel better about yourself, not worse, while you are with your spouse.

Doubting reality

Sure, you are trapped in their delusional world is one of the narcissist's main objectives, and to achieve this, they will need to keep you cut off from the actual world. This leads to the individual having a life where the fact is that everyone else is living a life that you deem questionable. You'll discover that you're perplexed.

It resembles a love triangle nearly exactly.

To scare you even more than before, the narcissist can accomplish this by establishing a love triangle and introducing a third-party dynamic into the relationship. By doing this, the abuser might further the notion that the victim is unworthy. The victim then makes an effort to receive the love and attention they require, and you will always make an effort to attract the narcissist's attention to obtain what they desire.

Although some of you want to end the relationship, you're too afraid.

It is understandable to want to end a relationship when violence is still present. Even though the victim of abuse always decides when and whether to leave, they frequently talk themselves out of leaving or are too afraid to do so. You may be dealing with an abusive narcissist if you frequently find yourself considering ending the relationship but feel unable to do so.

Being alone

You will always feel alone if you are in a relationship with a narcissist, which is another negative consequence. Due to their extreme self-absorption, you may still be in a relationship with them, but you will often feel alone.

Being alone when you are connected to someone else can be emotionally draining since it makes you want to be alone all the time. When you are with a selfish person, you may feel lonely since he will not listen to you despite your efforts to bring up your problems.

You feel worn out without knowing why.

You may feel worn out by the narcissist's emotional abuse. Feeling worn out is the most obvious sign that your relationship with them is going through an emotional rollercoaster. If you experience exhaustion that you are unable to adequately explain, it may indicate that you are in a relationship with a narcissist.

You are acting in a way that does not align with your interests.

A narcissist can trick you into acting in ways that serve them instead of you. They act this way because, in their eyes, you are not generally equal to them, nor are your demands comparable to theirs. You should reassess your relationship if you discover that your actions are motivated only by the narcissist.

You discover your partner is lying to you.

Pathological liars can be narcissists. They lie because they have demands and wants that can't be satisfied if they don't lie. For instance, a narcissist might lie to you to obtain something from you, such as money or attention. By lying, they can obtain items they would not be able to obtain if their partner acted rationally. The narcissist's entire façade is frequently false.

Separating or Distancing

Dissociation is a coping strategy when you distance yourself from your feelings. You often feel the need to completely separate yourself from your emotions to survive because they are so overwhelming for you. This is a common observation in survivors of traumatic events like rape or war, as well as in victims of narcissistic abuse. This is your mind trying to separate the abuse from you as the only way it can handle it. If you don't get help for this, it can lead to some very significant mental health issues. It may cause altered states of consciousness, interfere with your memory, and have major negative effects on your health.

Having No Faith in Anyone

You could react by becoming highly suspicious of those you formerly trusted and loved as a result of experiencing such severe abuse. You might always be on edge, fearing that you'll be deceived or harmed once more, and you might find it difficult to form lasting connections. Rather, you continue to be extremely cautious around other people, which just makes anxiety worse and creates barriers between you and other people. After your trauma, you probably believe that people, even those you have never had cause to distrust, are capable of hurting you.

Fearful Frequently or Consistently

Experiencing such complete betrayal, you can live in continual terror of the abuse happening again. If you have fled, you might worry that your abuser will find you again or that any happiness you experience is only a mirage. You have probably encountered obstacles to enjoying life on multiple occasions because narcissists have a propensity to punish those who make them happy. This has only contributed to your anxiety whenever things go well. You live in constant terror of the narcissist setting you off or of the other shoe dropping and shattering your fleeting moment of happiness. You could grow afraid of enjoying yourself, and as a result, you let the narcissist keep being the only one who has joy in life. The narcissist finds pleasure in witnessing his victims' fear of living fully.

Self-defeating

When you self-sabotage, you look for ways to keep yourself from reaching your goals. This is frequently connected to the narcissist undermining your sense of self-worth. You start to act out the narcissist's assertions about your skills because you start to believe them. If you hear the same thing repeatedly—that you're stupid—you'll start to believe it and act accordingly. Even though you're intelligent, your decisions will be driven by your sense of value. Self-sabotage can also take the shape of not taking the required actions to give yourself the independence you desire, making it impossible to leave the relationship when you want to.

Imagine Your Boss Is a Narcissist. What Then?

Managing a boss who exhibits narcissism might present additional challenges and nuances.to handle this circumstance in a way that safeguards your health and fosters a more positive work environment:

Record and evaluate the circumstances:

Record instances of narcissistic conduct from your boss before you act. Consider these actions' impact on you, the group, and the workplace. Collect unbiased proof of their actions, such as emails, messages, or recordings, to give your observations a strong basis.

Seek Out Assistance and Address Issues with Coworkers:

Consult with dependable coworkers and enlist their assistance. Inquire whether they have seen the supervisor acting similarly and if they would be willing to testify or discuss their experiences in private. Having the backing of several individuals might bolster your argument and demonstrate that the issue isn't unique to you.

Analyze the Business Environment:

Evaluate the support offered by upper-level leadership and the corporate culture. Suppose higher management condones or even encourages your boss's selfish behavior. In that case, you may need to take more serious measures to safeguard your emotional health, such as looking for alternative employment opportunities.

Put the facts and productivity first:

When speaking with your supervisor, pay attention to the details and output. Refrain from engaging in heated debates or confrontations. When speaking with your supervisor, make an effort to act professionally and results-oriented.

Establish definite boundaries:

Set firm limits on your supervisor's actions that you will not put up with. When communicating your boundaries, do so courteously and forcefully. Protecting yourself and your mental well-being is vital in a stressful work situation.

Think About Using Human Resources (HR):

You can consider contacting the company's HR department or human resources if your boss's actions are hurtful and detrimental to your performance and well-being. Give them official documentation of the boss's actions and ask for assistance in handling the matter properly.

Examine Your Career Options:

You might have to consider changing careers if you can't stand the narcissistic boss any longer and things don't get better. Changing a boss's conduct is not always possible, so your emotional and professional health should come first. Look into several employment options where you may showcase your skills and abilities to the fullest.

Organizational Psychological Assistance: If your position with a narcissistic boss is particularly tough, you may want to think about getting psychological help from a psychologist or psychotherapist. You can ask the HR department to find out if you can speak with an occupational health specialist to evaluate your stress level.

Recall that handling a narcissistic employer demands thoughtfulness and self-care. Keep track of incidents, ask for help, establish limits, and weigh your options. You have the right to work in a supportive and healthy atmosphere, and your health should always come first.

Here are some words you can use to improve things with your boss while you're at it. I usually advise using email to steer away from face-to-face interactions.

"I would like to enhance our collaboration and communication. Could we plan a meeting to discuss how we can work better together as a team?"

"I've noticed that sometimes ideas are dismissed without being fully considered. Could we dedicate some time to explore these proposals to see if they can lead to interesting solutions?"

"I would like to understand the context and objectives behind some of the decisions made. Could you explain how these choices were reached so I can grasp the bigger picture?"

"I would appreciate more specific feedback about my work. Could you help me better understand my strengths and areas where I can focus on improving?"

"I would like to be more involved in team projects and initiatives. Could we explore how I can contribute to the company's success in a more meaningful way?"

"I highly value your skills and talent. I also want the opportunity to contribute my unique skills and abilities to the team. How can I bring out my potential?"

"I would appreciate more transparency regarding decision-making processes and company goals. Clarity and understanding of directives would help me work more effectively."

"I've noticed that some of our meetings seem to focus only on certain ideas or suggestions. Could we try to involve the entire team to get diverse perspectives?"

"I feel motivated when my efforts are recognized. Positive recognition could be a great boost to my productivity."

"I would like more autonomy in my role and to make significant decisions. Could we explore how we can find a balance between your guidance and autonomy in my work?"

Always remember that your interactions with your supervisor should be civil, businesslike, and solution-focused. Employing email can give you a written record of your correspondence and allow your supervisor some thought before answering. The intention is to start a productive conversation that will help the business and you both.

Make Use Of Externalization's Power

The huge jump is the following step. Now that they know they have the option, some folks might be eager to start over. But before you can proceed, you must clear out all the toxins from your life.

You need to relearn some things, including learning to appreciate yourself for who you are and clearing out all the toxicity that has been stacked against you over the years.

Here are some ideas to assist you in the removal of all those toxins. These methods have been referred to as externalization, the reverse of internalization.

· Always be moving

It is simple to want to stay at home and feel sorry for yourself when you are in pain. Sulking is a tempting alternative because it's simple. All you need to do is spend the entire day in bed. Consume everything in the refrigerator and lead a lazy life.

You must get out of bed and possibly leave your home. According to studies, those who exercise for at least two hours a week would see a decrease in their risk of developing depression in comparison to those who lead sedentary lives.

But remember, it's acceptable to be depressed over all the negative things that happened to you with your narcissistic mother. So be free to grieve at your own pace. But you should also schedule some time to walk outside and get fresh air.

Depression is exacerbated by spending the entire day at home moping about your circumstances. According to one study, people who do it have a 44% chance of being depressed. Stretching is a good place to start.

In that manner, you won't need to leave the house just yet. You might also give yoga a shot. If you have a treadmill, then use that. Exercise for 15 to 30 minutes daily will have tremendous benefits for you.

It doesn't have to be a fitness regimen or something similar. Even better, just locate a music video and start dancing to it. The most crucial thing is to move, exercise, and enjoy yourself while doing whatever you're doing.

- Stroll

Make it a routine to work out for 15 to 30 minutes each day. The next thing you can do is start walking after that. Put on your headphones, turn on your preferred tunes, and take a blocklong stroll.

While exercising is fantastic, you're still confined to a small area. That restriction can trick your mind. Spending a week or more at home may make your mind a bit too full. Therefore, the answer is to broaden your mental horizons by traveling beyond your home.

I advise you to take your walks in places where you can connect with nature, such as parks or neighboring woodlands. Nature is a tremendous healer of emotions. Spending time in nature can lessen stress, fear, and rage. It will also make you feel better and improve your physical health.

In addition, I advise you to take walks in areas where you can spend some time by yourself thinking. Recall that your goal is to increase the size of your mental space.

Here's another advice:

Go for a stroll and speak to yourself positively.

While you're at it, speak to yourself.

Release all of your resentment.

Take in the wonders of Mother Nature by looking around you.

Exercise, and walking in particular, reduces feelings of melancholy and depression. According to a BBC news piece that cited medical reviews as one of its primary sources, taking a quick walk can help prevent depression.

Furthermore, engaging in self-talk while strolling is an excellent method of self-care. Compassion for oneself can be evoked by talking to and listening to oneself.

You might eventually find yourself sobbing uncontrollably over it once more. Just let it all out when that occurs. Allow all of your pain and suffering to fade. However, you should also recognize that, even after the grief has been released, a loving cosmos lets you know that your life is just as big as the space in front of you.

• Employ positive affirmations

Use everyday affirmations that you can tell yourself. When you first get up, you can get started on it. You can repeat these to yourself while brushing your teeth and gazing in the mirror.

A book of affirmations is something you can buy, but it's not necessary. For your phone, you can even download an app that allows you to read or even hear the affirmations uttered.

You must read the content or listen to it carefully. Even better, you can record yourself saying these sample affirmations.

I cherish who I am.

I'm a powerful female.

I've made it through.

I'm able to break up with my narcissistic mother.

I am a kind person, in contrast to my mother.

Without assistance from my mother, I can take care of myself.

Once more, this is an example of constructive self-talk. You may keep telling yourself it until you realize that you genuinely believed it in the first place. You are the only one who truly loves you. Something about hearing your voice comfort you from the inside out when it's telling you what you need to hear

- Keep a journal.

Others advise making journaling a regular habit. It's a means for you to release all of the hurt and frustrations from your relationship with your egotistical mother.

But if you do this, I advise you to write your diary entries as though you would like someone to read them at some point in the future. Compose your entries to help someone going through similar hardships by sharing what you have learned on those pages.

Write them with the intention of inspiring hope in the lives of others. You never know who might come across it years down the road. In the coming months, who knows who might be reading your entries—your son, your grandchildren, or even you?

Your journal will function similarly to a time capsule. You will occasionally come face to face with the hurt and pain you experienced. When they occur, though, you can always read back over your journal to see how you managed to find hope despite the suffering. Follow the guidance you provided to yourself months or years ago. Next, evaluate your progress and growth to see how far you have come.

An excellent way to start meditation is through writing. Your thinking will be erratic if you have recently experienced something traumatic. Your mind will be overtaken by recollections of your suffering, which may occasionally prevent you from meditating effectively.

You can experience a slowdown when you put things in writing. Recall that the hand writes more slowly than the thought. You can then concentrate on one event in your life at a time. Proprioceptive advantages can come from journaling. It may facilitate the reactivation of long-forgotten memories that you have suppressed. It's an opportunity to relax, let go of all the pain, and finally let your spirit heal.

Consider her an outsider rather than your mother.

What image of a lovely person who would stop at nothing to ensure you were okay comes to mind when you think of a mother? Because of this, it can be highly perplexing when they behave in an entirely inconsistent way with your expectations. This is true, especially when you contrast your life with your friends or with what you see on TV. Not only may this be confusing, but it can also make you quite angry.

You must adjust your perspective of them to cease perceiving them as something they are not and continue feeling perplexed and irritated. Rather, classify her as just another non-motherly woman. You'll start to recognize your connection for what it is in this way.

Establish Limits

Narcissistic mothers typically disregard all of your boundaries. They feel no regret when they cross them. However, this only persists because you are unaware of your bounds.

Instead, establish your boundaries and recognize when they are not being upheld. It's not enough to just set boundaries; you also need to learn to stick with them and treat them respectfully.

If you are an adult already, this is a wise choice. If you want to have a healthy connection with your mother free from codependency, then that is your best option. Establishing boundaries is telling people up front what you will and won't tolerate. It also enables children to comprehend where you stand and that you are creating a boundary that they must respect and remain inside.

Setting limits out of fear of upsetting their narcissistic mother is a common fear shared by many of their kids. Children may also be afraid of being abandoned, which is another reason they may be reluctant to set limits with their mothers. Although it makes sense that you wouldn't want to lose your mother entirely, taking this step is essential.

Narcissists usually allow individuals in and out of their lives because they believe there is no such thing as a middle ground. There are only two ways to see people: well and badly. But you must understand that when she emotionally abandoned you, you experienced the worst kind of sorrow. Abandonment in person won't cause you as much suffering. This implies that she is powerless to take any action that would result in agony equivalent to yours.

Setting limits is something you alone are capable of doing. It can benefit your long-term physical and mental health if you figure out how to approach it properly.

Assume Leadership

Many kids of narcissistic parents eventually realize they are being mistreated. They know that their lifestyles are not ideal, but they are unsure how to alter them. If this is the case for you, you must realize you are fully in charge of your feelings and emotions. Being the greatest version of yourself is necessary, rather than waiting for someone to assist you with your circumstances.

Recognize That It Could Be Logical to Move On

Keep in mind that sometimes you can't make your narcissistic mother behave differently. You can keep trying, but eventually, you'll realize nothing will change. When you take a step back, you'll eventually be able to recognize the connection for what it is. You might eventually run out of options and have to walk away.

How Do They Manipulate Humans?

Narcissists use a variety of the manipulative techniques we just studied to keep individuals under their control. Some narcissists might only use a handful, while others might use them all. Recall that narcissists are sophisticated individuals who can adapt their tactics to suit the person they are interacting with. If the person exhibiting narcissistic behavior in your life is a parent, such as your mother or father, they have probably used every tactic in the book. They will do everything in their power to idealize themselves and turn you into their dependent since they most likely have been abusing you since you were a small child. When you become reliant on someone, you have few choices and frequently have to satisfy them to satisfy your needs. Many of the manipulation techniques we discussed entail the narcissist using your closest relationships as leverage against you. Your perspective becomes warped, and you truly think that the narcissist is the only person who can love and care for you if you have no one to count on for support. If you can, consider your current narcissistic circumstances. Which techniques of manipulation does your abuser employ? You can gradually reject the narcissist's manipulation to stop narcissistic abuse by figuring out which manipulation technique they frequently employ.

Negative narcissism

Before, all we had studied about NPD patients' symptoms and diagnoses were their symptoms. It's well known that narcissists feel 'grandiose' and have an exaggerated sense of who they are; most of them are also unaware of the wrongness of their actions, which makes it challenging to persuade them to seek treatment. Nevertheless, I also wanted to educate you about the darker side of NPD. This area has the highest hostility, antisocial behavior, and suspicion levels. Malignant narcissism is the term for this kind of narcissism.

Malignant narcissism can ruin entire communities, including families, nations, and workplaces. The combination of antisocial and narcissistic personality disorders is known as malignant narcissism. People who have malignant narcissism can develop relationships and bonds with others, yet the way their brain processes information is from a position where they injure society as a whole. On the other hand, many individuals adore and rely on them. Individuals who are close to a malignant narcissist frequently have to tread carefully to protect their delicate egos and downplay their erratic and aggressive actions. These individuals may include family members, coworkers, and employees.

Even the slightest transgression will cause malicious narcissists to ridicule or attack others. For example, you would have shown confidence if you had spoken an opinion that differed from your malignant narcissistic mother's. She most likely turned around due to this, and she may now attempt to punish you by acting aloof or hostilely or insulting you to win back her trust. Some narcissists will go to great lengths to fabricate false information about themselves to realize their grandiosity and preserve their brittle sense of self. They could get upset if you refute their falsehood with data or proof. Because of the potential for "gaslighting," this behavior pattern frequently causes many issues for those close to them.

People frequently experience feelings of intimidation, fear, and anxiety when around individuals with malignant narcissism. Many people can suffer greatly from the deadly trifecta of hypersensitivity, suspicion, and aggressiveness combined with insufficient empathy. People who have contact with these types of narcissists will describe them as furious, crafty, nasty, punishing, thin-skinned, petty, and envious. They typically hold radical opinions and cannot control their emotions due to their superficial nature. The people around them suffer as a result of their decision-making processes. They frequently use flimsy criteria and classifications to rate the quality of their interactions with others. Their constant desire for dominance may make them appear selfless to maintain an advantage over others. They frequently have a very black-and-white, basic perspective on the world. People are wealthy or impoverished, successful or unsuccessful, attractive or ugly, etc. Despite all of this, they continue to believe that they are better than everyone else. The research we just covered suggests that this is most likely related to their brains' inability to interpret emotional information and defective neurobiology.

They are insecure: Individuals with NPD experience intense insecurity, which is the primary cause of their belief that demeaning others will boost their ego and satisfy their sense of entitlement.

Those who find narcissists appealing and beautiful find it strange to assume that they are insecure.

When a narcissist is susceptible, their uncertainty stems from their doubting whether they are truly exceptional and singular. They rely on praise from others to elevate their emotions of entitlement and greatness.

Low self-esteem characterizes narcissists. Their constant need to prove themselves drives them. They demonstrate their worth not only to themselves but also to others. This is a source of anxiety and inadequacy sentiments.

People with NPD frequently "fish for compliments" from others by boasting and bragging about their accomplishments due to their low self-esteem and insecurities. Put another way, they are adept at complimenting themselves while seeking praise from others (Seltzer, 2013).

Narcissists need an excessive amount of protection for their fragile and overblown egos, which can make them defensive and self-righteous. Their always vigilant defense mechanism is simply triggered with minimal effort. Not only do persons with NPD respond negatively to criticism, but they also react negatively to ANY action or statement that they believe casts doubt on their talents. Their defensemechanisms may become active as a result.

It is very difficult for persons with NPD to say they are wrong or have made a mistake and apologize since they believe that this is necessary for their survival.

Wrath is the reaction to opposing ideas. Narcissists find it difficult to accept being shown "wrong" and will often display their wrath this way. When someone feels humiliated or hurt from anything that happened in the past, they express their wrath as a reaction to these unwelcome emotions.

People with NPD are compelled, deep down, to conceal any shortcomings or imperfections in their self-image. As a result, they project characteristics and behaviors that they simply cannot or will not accept in themselves. As a result, they take any criticism of themselves and turn it towards other people.

Put differently, when someone with NPD is evaluated as being mean, bad, or incorrect, they will respond by saying, "I'm not mean, bad, or wrong; you are."

Their aspirations and aims: While having aspirations is generally admirable, narcissists carry their aspirations and goals too far. They have unending aspirations and goals, believe they are exceedingly unique and superior to everyone else, and dream of accomplishing more and being better than everyone else.

Their fantasies center on how much more powerful and wealthy they will grow to be and how much better they will be able to fulfill their dreams and surpass everyone else.

They will only socialize or converse with people they believe to be prestigious and well-known because of their sense of entitlement and superiority. They'll also get obsessed with status symbols, such as the posh automobile they drive, their neighborhood, or any private clubs they might be a member of. People who they don't think are on the same level or possess the same "status symbols" will be mocked and denigrated by them.

They can be charming - First impressions of establishing a

relationship with a narcissist, whether romantic or friendship, begin with them being their most confident and charming, a delight to be around and get to know. The difficult part is the "get to know" phase, as you'll probably want to "un-know" them once you truly get to know them.

Eventually, the narcissist's behavior in the relationships becomes aggressive, self-centered, demeaning, and easily agitated. They enjoy having authority over others and relish the power that comes with it. Once they have this status, they will use their influence over others to achieve their desires. They become irrational when they don't get their way.

They are fiercely competitive - You read in Chapter 2 that teens with NPD traits are typically conceited and can be fiercely competitive. The adolescent will continue to show such symptoms if they reach maturity and continue to develop their NPD traits.

One of the typical signs of narcissism is competition. An NPD sufferer will stop at nothing to achieve their goals. A person with a narcissistic personality disorder is obsessed with winning; they see no middle ground; there are only winners and losers, and they don't hesitate to label others as "losers" to prove their superiority.

They are unable to recognize or appreciate the accomplishments of others because of their constant drive to win, or they are forced into a precarious position where they cannot demonstrate their superiority over their rival.

Grudges: Narcissists' façade of excessive confidence and indifference to the opinions of others is just that—a veneer. They truly worry about maintaining their "perfect, unflawed" self-image and are, in fact, quite sensitive. When someone makes fun of them or expresses disapproval of the narcissist's actions, they are not very pleased. They harbor resentment because they perceive these acts as "personal attacks" and as a result.

When someone with NPD feels slighted, they don't let it go or move on. They won't tolerate what they see as "attacks."

Relationship Dynamics

WHAT ARE THE FAMILY DYNAMICS WHEN A NARCISSIST IS INVOLVED?

A selfish person is prone to feel empty, flawed, and inept when they are a parent. They are also likely to experience worry and depression for no apparent reason. It is also usual for them to seek care later in life to settle marital troubles or emotional ailments. They frequently don't know the fundamental reason for their mental disorder, though. A family with one or both narcissistic parents is frequently hiding a great deal of pain. These households operate under unwritten rules. The children are taught the rules but never really get it, and they always get annoyed by it. These unsaid laws impede their emotional access to their guardians. The kids think they are invisible as a result, and they frequently do appear to be. Sadly, a controlling parent might exploit these unwritten rules to violate boundaries with their kids and resort to them when needed.

In this chapter, let's have a listen to what a narcissistic family sounds like. If a member of your family is bullying you due to narcissism, this could be helpful. Remember that no two families are the same and that there are frequently differing levels of conflict depending on how selfish the adults are.

Lack of boundaries: Narcissistic families have little boundaries. Emotions in children are viewed as unimportant. Private journals are read, and physical and emotional boundaries are rarely acknowledged. No one in a narcissistic household has a right to privacy.

Negative messages: Children of narcissistic parents are subjected to a constant barrage of verbal and nonverbal cues, which they frequently internalize. Typically, these signals sound something like "You don't measure up," "You're not good enough," or "What you do determines your worth, not who you are." For this reason, a lot of kids will do whatever it takes to please their controlling parents.

Toxic relationships among narcissistic cultures are typically not readily apparent from the outside. The dysfunction is usually quite obvious in cases of violent and dysfunctional families, but it can also be readily hidden in cases of social and mental violence. Furthermore, the drama is extremely damaging to kids if not shared with other adults.

In a narcissistic household, emotions are disregarded if they are not addressed. Children are never taught by their parents how to process or accept their emotions appropriately. Rather, they are informed that their feelings are unimportant and are trained to repress them. Parents who suffer from narcissism often lack emotional intelligence, which they transfer to their kids. Suppressing a narcissistic parent's feelings results in a family dynamic that lacks integrity and accountability, and in extreme situations, it can result in psychological illnesses.

When people are not taught how to process their emotions appropriately, they may react in undesirable ways. The secret with narcissistic families is that the parents never give in to their kids' needs. Additionally, they treat them disrespectfully and verbally. In a home run by narcissists, this is the norm. The kids are taught that they can't let the outer world know about their problems. The children have to behave like a normal, happy family. One parent is the narcissist, while the other is the circling parent. The most common type of relationship involves a narcissistic parent and a needy spouse who will stop at nothing to keep the marriage intact. This other parent typically has a wealth of favorable traits that they can impart to their children. However, they frequently overlook the kids' needs since they spend much time and energy attending to their egotistical partner's demands. Sadly, for the kids to receive the love and care they so desperately need, they must grow up needing to satiate all of their parents' needs.

Chapter 4: Identify Your Stressors

Being conscious of your triggers is the first step towards ceasing to be a narcissist and to cease acting in selfish ways, such as dominating other people.

How to Identify the Triggers of Your Narcissism

First of all, you always act out of narcissism when you are provoked by something. This includes manipulative tears, narcissistic fury, humiliating a loved one, and silent treatment.

World-renowned Gestalt therapy expert Elinor Greenberg, Ph.D., CGP, instructs other psychotherapists in the diagnosis and treatment of personality disorders, including Schizoid Personality Disorder, NDP, and borderline personality disorder.

According to her, everything that makes you feel deeply bad about yourself to the point that you act out to correct your sense of self-worth is a trigger for narcissistic behaviors.

For example, you are likely to act out when your partner does something that annoys you. This "something" could be pointing out that a certain outfit detracts from your appearance rather than enhances it. Because the statement has damaged your brittle ego and self-esteem, you can become aggressive in such a scenario.

As triggers are the events or situations that set off your narcissistic tendencies, such as belittling other people and narcissistic wrath, you must become acutely aware of them to begin your journey toward narcissistic liberation.

The first step in doing this is to get out your notebook and list all the words, events, actions, and scenarios that make you act narcissistically towards the people in your life, only to later regret it. Right now, don't worry about the specifics; just write in a free-form manner about what makes you feel bad and want to act out violently against someone you think has said something that has damaged your self-esteem.

Your trigger list can resemble this:

When a "low status" person poses difficult questions, particularly ones whose solutions you are unsure of

When a "low status" person, like a "waiter" or "repairman," doesn't show you respect or doesn't serve you "fast as someone of your high caliber deserves."

When your significant other disregards you

When someone disagrees with you rather than regards it as a divine mandate

It's a good thing that paying more attention to yourself will make you more conscious because it is the first step towards conquering narcissistic tendencies.

You can use the following tactics to increase your awareness of the things that set off your narcissistic tendencies or behaviors, in addition to noting your triggers in your self-development notebook in a free-form manner.

#: Recognise Your Emotional Stressors

You can handle the truth now that it is here, right?

You are more likely to act narcissistically because of internal factors than external ones. These are known as emotional triggers.

You act narcissistically towards something (or someone) that you find offensive not because you constantly find the situation disagreeable but because you believe or feel the situation offensively.

This means that you react narcissistically to situations or people that don't make sense to you or fit your preconceived notions. Emotional triggers are the things that make you feel something or someone has injured you emotionally and damaged your delicate ego. This is why you react the way you do.

You can control your reactions by increasing your awareness of your emotional triggers, how particular objects and circumstances make you feel, and how you respond when you experience these things. You can't control something you don't know about, after all.

It's important to remember that everything that makes you feel bad and makes you want to react violently is what matters when determining which emotions set off your narcissistic tendencies. Emotional triggers that are frequently found to result in narcissistic behavior include:

Thanks to Margaret Paul, Ph.D.

You must get a deep awareness of your emotional triggers before you can quit being a narcissist or acting narcissistically and give up the drive to dominate everything, including your relationships. The explanation for this is straightforward: although you may attribute your actions and reactions to outside factors, the reality is that your feelings and emotions are ultimately responsible for your actions and reactions.

#: Pay Attention to How Your Body Is Feeling

If you pay close attention, you'll notice that your body responds to your emotions in a certain way when you're prepared to act narcissistically. When someone doesn't treat you like the "demi-god" you believe yourself to be; for example, you may experience tenseness in your body, rapid breathing, and an increase in body temperature, depending on how insulting you find the "insult." You can become more conscious of the different physical changes that take place before engaging in narcissistic behavior by paying attention to your body.

www.ingramcontent.com/pod-product-compliance
Lightning Source LLC
Chambersburg PA
CBHW052152110526
44591CB00012B/1957